EDITED BY MYRA COHN LIVINGSTON

Callooh! Callay!: Holiday Poems for Young Readers
(A MARGARET K. MCELDERRY BOOK)

Listen, Children, Listen: Poems for the Very Young

O Frabjous Day!: Poetry for Holidays and
Special Occasions
(A MARGARET K. MCELDERRY BOOK)

One Little Room, an Everywhere: Poems of Love
(A MARGARET K. MCELDERRY BOOK)

Poems of Lewis Carroll

Poems of Christmas
(A MARGARET K. MCELDERRY BOOK)

Speak Roughly to Your Little Boy: A Collection of
Parodies and Burlesques, Together with the Original
Poems, Chosen and Annotated for Young People

A Tune Beyond Us: A Collection of Poems

What a Wonderful Bird the Frog Are: An Assortment
of Humorous Poetry and Verse

No Way of Knowing

DALLAS POEMS

No Way of Knowing

DALLAS POEMS

Myra Cohn Livingston

A Margaret K. McElderry Book

Atheneum 1 9 8 0 New York

Library of Congress Cataloging in Publication Data

Livingston, Myra Cohn.
No way of knowing.
"A Margaret K. McElderry book."
SUMMARY: Poems based on the author's experiences
in the black community of Dallas, Texas, from 1952 to
1964.
1. Afro-Americans—Texas—Dallas—Juvenile
poetry. 2. Children's poetry, American. [1. Afro-
Americans—Texas—Dallas—Poetry. 2. American poetry]
I. Title.
PS3562.I945N6   811'.54   80-14584
ISBN 0-689-50179-X

Published simultaneously in Canada by McClelland & Stewart, Ltd.
Manufactured by American-Book Stratford Press, Inc.
Saddlebrook, New Jersey
Designed by Maria Epes
First Edition

To Arzetta with love

No Way of Knowing

DALLAS POEMS

He make me
like to split my sides
with laughing at his jokes.

He come around
on Sunday
when he visiting his folks.

He smell so
sweet with perfume
that I like to faint away

And he call
my name so soft and sweet
I ask him for to stay

And take a
plate of supper
and an extra piece of pie

And Mama
have a fit with me
and say she like to die

Before she
have that Albert
hanging round to be her kin

But I seen
her smile as big as me
when Albert, he walk in.

When Kennedy
Come to our town
He come with dreams
Got shot right down.

It rained all morning.
You can bet
They didn't want him
Getting wet.

They put a bubble
On his car
So we could see him
From afar.

But then the sun
Come out, so they
Just took the bubble
Clean away.

When Kennedy
Come to our town
Some low-down white folks
Shot him down,

And I got bubbles,
I got dreams,
So I know what
That killing means.

Time to go fishing
now it Spring

can't keep my mind
on anything

just hear that water
murmuring

down at the creek
where bullfrogs sing

fishes just
a-gathering

for all the worms
I dig to bring

and me, real quiet,
reckoning

a *beaucoup* of catfish
bouncing my string.

✸ ARZETTA TO ED

No way
I'm gonna
sweet talk you

no matter
what you say or do

Big Boy,
I tell you
straight ———

We through!

I be thinking
of that day
Minnie upped and
gone away,

took her purse
and disappear.
Ain't seen her now for
most a year.

Once she phone
and say she fine
and seeing how she
blood of mine

she tell me of
her loving man
and they come back soon
as they can

and bring the baby
home to me
and what a real fine
boy he be,

and how we gonna
laugh again
when she come home with
her two men.

And I be thinking
time she come
so things don't be so
worrisome.

But sun come up
and moon go down
and still she don't come
back to town

and all this time
I wonders why.
What cause my Minnie
got to lie?

my boss man say
new times is here,
done served him
for a heap of years;
done did my job
the most I could,
done my masseusing
like I should,

but now come time
to go away
and rest a spell,

my boss man say.

This here
dirt just
gotta go,

Bessie frown
and Bessie know.

Put a
kerchief
on her head,

Beat that dirt
until it dead.

That much
better,
Bessie say

as she smile
and walk away.

that man crazy
in the head
think he gonna run this show

think he gonna boss me round,

what *I* thinking
he don't know.

that man fixing
for a fight,
that man never going to win,

that man better watch hisself,

that man never
do *me* in.

BOBO

Bobo join the Navy,
say
it real good work,
it real good pay

and send us cards keep saying when
he come to visit us again

leastways if he get two-week leave
and we not going to believe

the things he seen,
fine times he had ———

but since he left
our times been bad.

Cora's parlor
look so fine,
silver gleam,
china shine,
look around most anywhere,
fancy doilies on the chair,
lacy curtains on the door,
big soft rug down on the floor,
lots of pictures on the wall;
Cora Sally say it all
what she save out of her pay,
buys it all in layaway.
Mr. Sally done allowed
what she bought sure make him proud.

It Mr. Sally, Cora smile,
make her pretties all worthwhile.

✺ ED

Ed like to fish,
get him a pole
and dig a hole
and sit and wish
he catch a pail
of silver brim
and then land him
a yellowtail
from out that creek
so all the week
he fish and fry
what swim on by

until he pull
a bellyfull

Possum caught in the garbage can;
Big a possum as you can find.
Ms. Hall say to leave it there,
Not to pay it never mind.

Trouble is, she never know
Just how good that possum be.
Takes it out and cooks it up;
Got a whole week meal for me.

Ms. Hall, she say, "Georgie, how
You think that possum run away?"
"Well ma'm," I just tells her true,
"Don't rightly know if I can say

But late last night I hears a noise;
Something lifts that lid right off
And steals that possum clean away."
Ms. Hall, she be fit to cough

And walk away and keep herself
Clear of the kitchen three whole days.
We been together twenty year
And Ms. Hall, she done know my ways.

Hubert come at lunchtime,
White whiskers on his face —

Reckon there a little work
be done about this place?

Good at patching screens, he say,
Good at hanging doors.
Seem your windows like to streak.
Polish up them floors?

Hubert know no work we need.

Mama raise her head
and tell him to go feed the birds

and give him cheese and bread.

Devil, he know
All lost sinners.
Show them heaven
Far away.

Closest place is
Brimstone, ashes —
Come along here
Boy, he say.

See the Devil
Every evening
Gambling, swearing
Where I go.

Tell him, Man,
You get behind me.
Take it easy —
Take it slow —

Don't you mess with
Me, you Devil,
This sad earth done
Paid you well.

Took my Daddy,
Took my brothers,
Keep you laughing
Down in Hell.

❂ LENNIE

Reckon
I   can
spit
far   as   my Daddy
if I've a mind to

and my mind

                    up

just made itself

only know I loved you
Daddy
watched you
hoping someday
maybe
me and you'd
do things real
crazy
always hoped
you'd call me
baby —

didn't see
that things were
shabby
couldn't tell
things went so
badly
never knew
you were
unhappy
only knew I loved you
Daddy

Won't Lettie's baby
Be surprised

When they get her
Christianized?

Pour the water
On her head

Get her to heaven
When she dead.

LOUIS

Only person call me Honey
be my Louis, passed twelve years.
I be living still with fears
how he look so poorly, bony,
while I scrapes around for money
and near drowns myself in tears
while he like to fill my ears
with his sweet talk — Honey. Funny
how his voice come now to grieve me
busting through that mouth of spittle,
don't hear nothing in that call
saying he'd be like to leave me,
even through the last death-rattle.
Don't seem fair to me at all.

✻ MARLA

No telling what
that
Marla do.

She outa sight
before
we through

with dinner
or
the dishes done.

Don't think
of anything
but fun

and making
eyes
at every man

and getting home
late
as she can.

Wish I could
do
what Marla can.

Got me a special place
For Martin Luther King.
His picture on the wall
Makes me sing.

I look at it for a long time
And think of some
Real good ways
We will overcome.

Mattie,
she says
long ago

Black folks
full of
hurt and woe.

Times
have changed now,
so she said.

Mattie
crazy
in her head.

MINNIE

Lace sure favor Minnie.
Make her look so bright.
She been luring me along
Since we first dance tonight.

No question she the spider.
No question I the fly.
No way I gonna miss that web
When Minnie spin on by —

MISS DAISY LEE

Next thing I know
Miss Daisy Lee
crooked her finger right at me.

Come here, boy,
she sort of hissed.
Looks like here a place you missed

cleaning
and I pays you good
so windows sparkle like they should.

Fetch that pail
and wash it now
so all them streaks don't show nohow.

Don't understand
Miss Daisy Lee
who has to lay the blame on me

when yesterday
I heard her tell
how all her windows look just swell

and she'd be
telling folks she knew
to let me clean their windows too.

I like Miss Daisy,
except that she's
just a mite too hard to please.

When Billy passed,
Miss Stanley made
Four great big jugs of lemonade

And ham and cookies
And a cake
Took her two hours for to bake.

Miss Stanley say
It give her joy
To ease the grief of that poor boy

And see him safe
And out of pain
And never have to hurt again

And she be proud
To come around
When Billy laid into the ground

And see us eat
The things she made
And drink her bitter lemonade.

Never can remember
which of those
three Kings
was Black.

Jaspar?
Balthazar?
Melchior?

Doesn't matter, I guess,
Long as it was one of them.

lightning
strikes the sky
again

and heads down right at me

thunder
booms the earth
and when

it looks to hit the tree

I run
and pull the covers
back

and jump into the bed

and I
say more prayers
than

anyone at Meeting ever said.

Netta
buy an upright piano

Make her
proud as anything

Say she
like to take ten lessons

Learn her
how to play and sing

Make her
payments every Friday

Say in
three year it be hers

Nothing
like a fine piano

Netta
say, to ease her nerves

OLA: AT THE DANCE

First she flutter up her eyes
like she seen a big surprise.

Then she make herself real small
like she scared of seeming tall.

Next she scrunch around a bit
like her dress don't want to fit.

Then she give a mighty sigh
and make like she be sweet and shy

while all the time her eyes moves fast
fixing on the boys go past

until she get her first big chance
when some boy ask her up to dance.

Right off she hold his hand real tight
and make her teeth shine big and bright

flashing everyone a smile
like she been dancing all the while

and lean her head so cute and coy
and hold real tight on to that boy

he thinking *he* the one to lead ——

What Ola got, no boy don't need.

Plays me lots of tunes
on my mandolin
of all the places
I done been

in Lousiann
where Spanish moss
drag down the trees
like it be boss

and the bayous running
along the road
and cotton pickers
with their load

of that soft, white stuff
thrown on their backs;
black sweating bodies
in flour sacks

and a whole heap more
of things I knew
before the old
turned into new

but it seem like
a hundred year ago,
and the young folks laughs
at what Simon know.

Seen him
slick his hair back
when he think
I gone to play.

Seen him
raise his chin way up
to shave
no beard away.

Seen him
tighten up his belt,
throw out
his skinny chest,

smoothing
at his eyebrows
and pretending
he all dressed

up fancy,
strutting round the room
like he was
really cool.

Make me wonder
what dumb gal
he think
he gonna fool?

❋ ROBERT

Trouble,
he
my enemy

always
come
to pester me

messing
up
what I begun

slapping at
me
when I done

telling
packs
of doggone lies

reckon
he
don't realize

I knows
him
from day of birth

knows
his
footsteps on this earth

knows
he
joy to hassle me —

Trouble,
he
my enemy.

Rosa tapping
    at the window
    with her quarter,
    tapping hard,
    hoping some sweet man will see her;
    step inside our rundown yard,
    ring the bell and find her standing,
    smile painted on her face;

happen all the years I know of,
    lots of callers round our place.

Think of Rosa
    when I see a
    fancy woman
    dressed real fine;
    how she used to give me pennies,
    pat my head and say she mine.
    "Rosa tired," she would whisper,
    "you grow up, take care of me,

    fix the yard, put up new curtains,
    just us two keep company."

House not much to look at.
Need a coat of paint.
Some folks think it big inside.
I know it ain't.

Got too many kinfolk
like to make me mad
tearing up inside the house,
messing it bad.

Only thing done pleasure me —
the garden, fine and neat,
gardenias growing by the door.
Gardenias mighty sweet.

SALLY

got me a dress
and a new pair of shoes
dress is pink
and the shoes is white

dress real grand
for this fancy dance
make me look
such a pretty sight

put up my hair
and paint my lips
have a real good time
tonight

onlyest thing
they don't know
gonna dance without shoes
cause they too tight

just sit me down
and rest a spell
don't feel so well
I like to drown

with all the ache
most every day
just got to pray
Sweet Jesus, make

me right again,
my head real clear,
my blood to start

through all these veins,
hush up the fear
and joy my heart.

yeah,
I dig ya
yeah,
yeah,   And don't go thinking I don't.

yeah,
I like ya,
yeah,
yeah,   And don't go thinking I don't.

Way you walking suits me fine.
Way you talking makes you mine.

yeah,
I dig ya,
yeah,
I like ya   So don't you go thinking I don't.

TOM: EPITAPH

Tom come from Arkansas
far piece away.

Come here to find him work,
come here to stay.

Things fine for Tom for many a year,
no one to hassle him, no one to fear.

No way of telling all Tom been through,
no way of saying all old Tom knew,
no way of knowing all that Tom saw,

ain't no place like Dallas
for a boy from Arkansas.

Woodson
He drive everyday
Old Miss Bess to get his pay.

Sunday
He got afternoon
To rock on his porch and play him a tune.

Woodson
Say he fixing to quit.
Car no place for him to sit —

Streets
No place for man to be
Now he turning eighty-three.

Ada cooking up a storm

keep that kitchen powerful warm
with gumbo steaming in my eye
and chitlings just put on to fry,
biscuits piping hot and light
and greens with pork done up just right —

What ailing you, I asks her straight,
we got no chicken on this plate?
and I don't see no pie, no way —

Get outa here!
                    that's all she say ——

you come with me and
play a spell

cause we got things we
gonna tell

while we be having
us a walk

we got to have a
friendly talk

cause I know it be
me and you

can stick together
just like glue

and let your Mama
go away —

Good riddance — she too
old to play!

Sweet Jesus
He love Sundays
when we gather in his name

listening
to the preacher
be telling of the day

we brothers
and we sisters
lays all our troubles down

and Jesus
send His chariot
low and carry them away.

DATE DUE

MAR 0 3 '92			
APR 15 '97			
GAYLORD			PRINTED IN U.S.A.